# I got to be Here

Happy MIND Happy Life

# I got to be Here

Deb Stratton

First Edition
First Printing, 2017
Second Edition Printing 2020

I got to be here/ Deb Stratton/ Debbie S. Stratton/Buffum

ISBN- 9798680666111

Printed in the United States Of America

For Me-

And you

Because it is. Just that simple.

And My Mom

I can't imagine what you have been through. I know it must have been hard. Open your heart and realize that what you have been through has taken you down a path to this day. Today.

Here we are. There are many humans struggling with the thoughts of what they are here for and what their life purpose is. I am sure that you are one of the humans. Some live in a place of sadness. You know that place. It is the constant thoughts and distractions around you.

Many call it mind chatter. What will my brain tell me today? Will I be happy? Will I be enough? Am I living the life that I have always dreamed of?

What place do you live in?

A little bird told me you might be wondering what is going on.
I think it is time to be happy again, that is all. Being happy doesn't mean that everything is perfect, it just means you have decided to see life beyond the imperfections. Maybe I said that wrong. You may be happy. But not complete. Which means you're kind of happy but something is missing.
What is it?
I am sure we can find it here somewhere.

Here we go. Did I thank you for being

here? Thank you.
I am really glad that you stopped by. I wanted to spend some time with you and figure out some things. I have so many questions. I just can't seem to get it together lately. What is the real purpose of being here?

About me: I am just like you. Wanting more. Wanting to be happy.

If you are wondering what I look like, it is a little like this.
Perfectly Imperfect. How do you see yourself?
I am happy you are here.

# 1

The walking stick. Get it? It is a play on words. We are held together gently. Not only are we pieces but we also use one to walk with.

Not everyone will see the similarity. Close your eyes and look for it. You are alive and here. Any small thing can damage those sticks. Any large thing can cause you to depend on one.

The trick here is to put the concept together. We are here in this world. We are living and breathing. You have so much to offer other humans. I often see others making their mark in the world by giving and doing so much. They are so driven to do this that they forget to stop and give to themselves. You have a gift to give not only to others but to yourself.

I spend a tremendous amount of time trying to figure out the meaning of life. I want to know what my life is all about. I need to know which path to take and what will lead me to my ultimate idea of happiness.

That idea comes in many forms. It is sometimes a life filled with love. It is also the dream of having a home designed perfectly to my liking. I am surrounded by boxes of items that I have collected over the years that make me feel complete.

I need these things. They are mine. I want them. I want more. All of these things complete me in some fashion. They are a symbol of my desire to obtain items that are not mine and make them a part of me. I know that is a small way to think. I spend my days working towards getting every single thing I have ever desired. I want that. I really am going to get it. It will be mine.

Once it is mine, I can keep it forever. Or I can keep it as long as I want.

I am using my ability to capture my goals and dreams in a way that just keeps filling up my house. My life is not filling up. Just my closets and shelves.

I want to offer myself to the world. I got to be here! How lucky I am. Not everyone makes it. So here I am on this small planet floating around in a huge universe without a clue. I am here. Now what do I do? Everyone wants to make the world a better place. I also see and hear others say they want to change the world by offering their own contribution of love and money.

There is that word again. Money. Stuff. Love. It is a constant in everyone's life. We need it and want it. I could try to figure it out but that would take years. By the time I reach the grandest years I will be giving away the stuff that I spent my entire life wanting and getting. Why would I need that old stuff? I spent years at a job to buy those items only to spend most of my life at a job that kept me locked up from the outside world.

That job pulled me in more. It wanted more and more of my time. I stopped gardening. I stopped playing with the kids. I stopped sleeping on rainy days. I stopped laying on the ground and looking at the sky.

But I stayed there. I had to. If I did not stay at that job I would not get stuff. Then I would not be happy. I spent many days there just to get one day off to pick up the items I had thought about all week. I find the perfect place in my home to put it and leave it there. Just like everything else. It will be there in another week when I get one more day to be at home. If I am home. I just might be out picking up more stuff.

It is exhausting to make this dream come to life. I will work another month to get a few days off to clean my stuff. I may move it around. I could run out of room and put the stuff out for sale. Then I can make money and get new stuff. That stuff really is getting old anyway. Why would I want old stuff?

I am sure you are following me. We are here with our stuff right now. How does that make you feel? It makes me pretty darn happy. I love my stuff. As a matter of fact I am having a hard time writing this because I am looking up at my collection of items all around and want to envy it. Wow. I really have a lot of stuff. I worked so hard for all of it and missed the entire point of being here in the first place. I missed it all. Just to have this one moment with my stuff.

Relax. You are not alone if you are also looking at your stuff. Go ahead. Take a moment and glance over the top of this book and feel that warm feeling that comes. It is a feeling that makes us all stop in our tracks. We sit and think about life. When we do, it is often about what we want.

My path in life is certainly about this subject. I need my walking stick. My stuff is starting to weigh me down. I have a limp. I am broken. I have nothing figured out and time is going by quickly. All I have is this stuff.

But what about people? It is very similar. I need people. I need someone to love. I need someone to love me. I want to love a dog. I want to love chickens. I will feel complete when I have these things. I am filling myself up with stuff and love. That is good. I can put the stick away. All of that love made my frail limbs stronger. Wow. I really needed that.

I want to sit here for another moment. I look around and there are people around me. I have created these humans to bring love into my life. I sometimes worry that they do not have enough stuff. Again. That will make their life better. They need stuff. By giving it they will love me more.

I need this love and this stuff so much that I will go and work some more. I may work twice as much. Surely there will be a day when they have enough items filling up their lives that they will be happy. Their happiness turns into love for me. I am fulfilling my supreme destiny in life.

Right now by getting all of this and giving all of that. I am now not only collecting things but I am collecting people and an occasional animal along the way. This is making my existence meaningful and happy. I have followed my path in life over and over. It always leads to the same ending. Stuff. Love.

Somewhere out there though, there is a path we do not see yet. You know the one. It is not the light at the end of the tunnel in hard times. It is the path of becoming old. Oh that tunnel is something alright. It can be deadly. It can pull you in faster than anything and guess what? All of that stuff will not fit. There is barely any room to take the humans around you in it.

Hopefully you loved them enough and missed all of the years that you had on another path to give them the stuff. I cannot emphasize enough how important that was. They will never forget you. You will come up in their conversations for many years as the one that made them so happy. Do you remember when she got me that new car? Oh well I can beat that. Do you remember when she gave you all that she had and you gave it away. You had too much stuff. She spent years working to get it away from her own desires and yup. You sold it. You gave it to someone. Now she is stuck in that path nearing the end and she gave it all up for you.

The path gets shorter. The last path is so short that we spend a lot of time wishing that the other long paths we left behind would come back. I need that path I had when I was fifteen. Oh to be thirty again. I would have not worried so much about that stuff. Where is it anyway? I was sure I had it. I guess I left it somewhere. Maybe someone took it after I came down this new path. I must have been confused. I thought I needed it. I could not live without it.

The path is getting darker and the stuff is gone. The humans are gone. They are busy working to get their stuff. After all they need it. It is the only way to get to the last path.

Yes, I got to be here. I got the stuff. I lost it and got some love. I lost that too

when I did not have enough stuff to keep it.
I miss that the most.

# 2

If I give it to you don't break it. Get it. I am giving you heart so please be careful. In other words. Here is my love please do not trample on it. Do not mangle it or step on it. Just keep it in your heart. Carry it with you. Be grateful for it.

It is not that hard to care for it. It is easier than a hamster. You take it and love it. You give the love back. Maybe you want to give me your heart. I will gladly accept it.

Love is a funny thing. I may have heard that somewhere before. Love is patient, kind, forgiving and above all the most beautiful thing that has ever existed. I honestly believe that. Do you want some?

Some humans spend their entire lives searching for love. It is way more important than stuff. Some may not agree. Some may like their stuff way more. But here is the thing. You can have your cake and eat it too. Here it is. The cake. Take it. Do you love it? I want you to have a lot of cake in your lifetime. Cake and pie. Savor every single bite.

So here I am. Realizing again how lucky I am to have the experience of life. I love it. What does that say? Not only can you love someone but you can love the idea of something. You can love the feeling of something. I love the beach. I love my dog. I love my mom. Wow. You might say I am on a love overload. But not really. I have actually been alone for a very long time if you compare other humans' love experiences. I do not have someone in my life that tells me they love me. I miss that.

I made a decision years ago that no other human could walk down my path with me if they were going to hurt me. That means physically or emotionally. There can be no exception to this rule. It is my one true stand my ground rule.

If I give it to you please be gentle. I am afraid you may not be able to understand or comply. I hope the humans are being kind to you. If you are walking down a path with your stick and stumble you may want to whack that person that is hurting your heart. Do not let them stay in that space.

I can talk about the mushy gushy kind of love all day but really want to throw this out there. Love hurts. Oh wait I have heard that before also. But it does. It can suck. It can make you hate the life you were lucky enough to have. After all it is no accident that cells exploded and caused your cute little face to come into this world. Here you are. You get one chance. This is the only chance. I may repeat that once more. This is the only chance that you have to acquire love and stuff. But is that what you want? You are enough. It is really all about you. Just you.

Others may tell you differently. They may tell you that you can come back after you walk the last path. You may come back as a butterfly. The chances that you get to come back as another human that is similar to what you are now is slim. I may be wrong but how will you ever be able to prove it to me if you leave this world. Please try to send me a message and let me know. I will be waiting. Waiting to find out if I have a chance for a do-over. I need one.

Regardless of what you believe, here we are. I cannot cover or think about every mean and terrible situation in this world but I will tell you this. Some people are mean. They will hurt you. They will only think of themselves. They will never treasure your heart.

Guard your treasure. You are beautiful. It is just my thoughts but I am sure that I must be right in believing this. Someone may come along and throw your heart down to pick up another. It happens. They will not lose one night of sleep over the despair they cause you. They will move on to the next human and squeeze all of their love out also.

I am sure this will happen. The process is always the same. Eye contact. Attraction. Non stop thinking of this person. The need to give love and get it back. Whoops. There it is. They want you. What is next. Will they love you forever? Will they turn into someone else.

Here comes another one I have heard once.

**When a person shows you who they are, believe them the first time.**

Oh, yes. I hear this over and over. I met this great human. I felt so much love and then it was awful. It was horrifying. I lay crying on the floor naked all night. I wanted to jump off of the bridge. I cannot go on. They took my heart and forgot to give it back. Now I am without one. How will I ever find love again if I do not have one. I cannot buy one. I cannot borrow one. Maybe I can grow a new one. Maybe it will come back someday.

Why do I even want it? I am not sure where all of this is going anyway. I think I will start over. Unless you are still too busy looking at your stuff. I hope you send me photos of it.

I think what I am trying to say or think about is love. That four letter word that is the reason behind a lot of emotions. How can we go from path to path, person to person, and heart to heart?

I love you but I love them too. Some humans have so much love to give they want to love more than one person. Not just one person but multiple. They have a collection of hearts.

What does this mean? That human is not capable of love? Do they really know what the word or feeling means? How can we assume that because we believe love is supposed to be good and wonderful, that it is?

Maybe it is supposed to be dark and self centered. Or hurtful. That may be the experience that some may only know. Some humans may go from heart to heart trying to find their idea of love. We all have that image in our mind that tells us what love looks like. The perfect person is out there for everyone right? There has to be. The trick is finding them. Where the heck are they at?

Will they show up with a beautiful heart that is in disguise? They may make promises about the future that will never happen. The promises may be a way for them to get what they want which is usually not love. They may want material things or money. They may hurt others to build up their own self esteem. Whatever the reason may be guarding yourself against these types of people is not easy.

You're reduced to feeling like a smaller human because of these types of love. It can be an endless cycle because that person will always demonstrate that they are right. It is a dream killer. This person steals your joy and happiness. Learn to recognize it early and live a happy life filled with self love.

LOVE BEING IN LOVE BEING LOST IN LOVE FINDING LOVE FEELING LOVE LOVING YOURSELF LOVING LIFE WHERE IS THE LOVE I AM THE LOVE

Keep movin' on. Just keep on keepin' on.

You have to keep going until you get

it all figured out

If I go faster will you hold me
tighter?

The most beautiful words I have ever
heard.

It is all about the ride.
This is your one chance.
To live the moment that you have.

When that moment is here.
Take it.
Be grateful.
Thank yourself for being brave.
You did not sit in your room.
You went.
You smiled.
You were happy.

When that moment is gone grab another.
Enjoy being you and know that is the best
feeling.

**It may change your path.**

Words are so powerful.
Think of this.

Who are you when you are alone. When
no one else is there to see you. When
you have no one to impress.
That is the real you.
That is the you that you need to be
Everyday.

**I like wearing pajamas all day. I
don't make my bed. I dance to every
song I hear. I love to sing. I braid my
hair.**

**I am doing what is me.**

## Love yourself

Warm bath water. Flowers on the table. A breeze coming in through the window. Fresh sheets and quilts on the bed.

Do you see where I am going yet?

## Self care. Self love.

It is about to get deep around here. You got to be here. It is not selfish to care for yourself and who you are. It is not wrong to feel tired and worn out. Putting others before you is tiring and there needs to be a time in your life when you make the decision to love you. Love yourself. Fill yourself up with self love. It does not mean that you stop caring for others it just means that you will be always putting yourself first. Without you the world would be a lonely place.

You matter. Stop going without what you need to keep others happy and moving forward. I know you can do it. You are special and amazing.

Please do not change for others. Please do not forget who you are.

The most important thing that I have learned is that you will never be able to do enough or be enough to make others happy. You are enough of you to be perfect. At the very moment you realize this your life will change.

This is the hardest part.
You are perfect.
You have something to offer this world.

You may be bent but you are not broken.

You may be depressed but you are not giving up.

You were only given this life because you are strong enough to live it.

## You are a precious heart.

Take just a second to realize that right now no matter where you are or what you are doing that you are here. You are always at home.
You are always perfect.

Dig around inside of that house of yours. I will wait.
Move some of the stuff and oh yes! Right there! You found it! You found yourself! It was there all along. Right there with it there should be your heart. Keep looking. Wow. You sure have a lot of stuff. Move aside the boxed up feelings and boxes of sadness. They are no longer needed. What you are looking for is the box that says Today. Right now that box is all that you need. Those old boxes have been sitting around long enough. Why do you still them?

In a realistic setting. You could just run out and get some boxes. Put them in your room. Your kitchen. Write on them with your big marker. Label them with all of the things you still think about and worry about.

You may need quite a few. It may start to get a little crowded there. Keep going. Are you finding it hard to move around the house now? Moving those boxes of broken hearts, hurt feelings, lost friends, jobs, money, and sadness around will be exhausting.

Try to find a place to sit. I can hardly see you. Are you moving? It looks like you are sitting on the couch with a room full of dreams and broken dreams.
That is a lot.
Why is it so hard to just wake up and have the perfect day?
Because something is always missing.
Or something is always broken.

It is a constant.

But get this. You are at home in your heart. It is the place where you will always be. The room you are in. The place where you live. The life that you have. All of that is just surroundings. Home is inside of you. There is no room inside of you for all of those boxes. So why carry them around?

Let me help you carry them out. I worry that someone may take them and fill their lives with it. We must not set it out in the open.

# Ok.

Good. The boxes are gone. It is perfect now.
You are free now.

You are still you. You feel it?

Those things were keeping you boxed in.
They are gone now.
The clear path is ahead of you now.

No distractions. Look at yourself now.
You are free.

It is the moment you just see that now you will be ok.

The old drama is gone. The missing is gone.
The dreams get renewed.

## It all starts now.

Don't let it upset you. You may run back out and try to get the boxes back before the trash man comes. You might even sit in the room now and look around at how empty it is.

It may feel strange at first.

It will never matter what someone thought of you.
Or what you did not have.
Or what you had.
Or that someone hurt you.

You cannot let that mind chatter win.

It is time to wake up.
You have made it to this point because you were tired of those boxes. You spent too long moving them around.

It's exhausting.

But now you are ok.

Smile and know you are ok.
I love your smile.

**I have good days and I have days where I don't get what I want.**

The mind chatter is back. I am creating my own outlook. I am searching for what? I am having a good day only when I get what I want. It is all going back to the wanting and yes, you guessed it, stuff. I promise not to get started on that again. Even though I feel that I am still admiring the shelf of my favorite books. I am looking down at my shoes lined up by the door. Oh jeez I really love them.

Creating space for others while still taking care of yourself is on repeat mode. If you can think just for this moment about this you will see. You need to be reminded daily by your own self who you are. The freedom is there for the taking.

What are you waiting for? Grab it. Snatch it up. Take yourself to the happy and drama free life. Focus on you. Be you. Be really clear about what you want. Those days when you do not get it can be good also.

Look back up. It is only a good day when you get what you want. All days are good but some are better than others. I love it. I love the mornings when there is nothing right there to show me how my day will be.

All seems well. It is quiet and good. Then life happens. Something breaks. Someone creates gossip or drama that should not involve me. I worry about the bills. I worry about the kids. I worry about this and that. Then I created a morning filled with thoughts of uncertainty. How did that happen?

I just woke up! I am filled with self love and caring. I am showing love for others but still keeping me first. It was beautiful out and I had all of my stuff. And the mind chatter began. Out of nowhere. It came and turned my day into something unexpected. My good day could be better. If I let it. Why not let the day turn into a wonderful day filled with thoughts of gratitude? Oh that would be too easy.

It is much too easy to use the mind to create a peaceful and perfect life. There is too much going on around us. It gets easier. Put the plan into place to keep your thoughts positive and clear. You know this day is the one that is still on the path where you are ok. Hopefully it is not your end path. So there is still time. I would say the time is now. Maybe this book should be a few less pages so you can get out there and enjoy it all.

Go ahead if you need to. Fold down the little corner on this page and put the book down. Look out the window. Go outside. If you are working, find a way to take more time for yourself. Use that time up to enjoy this beautiful world. You would be surprised to know how many humans are actually starting to do that.

Spending all of that time at work for all of that stuff is not really taking care of you is it? Put on that shirt you never wear because you are saving it. Put your favorite song on and dance. Are you getting it?

I will wait right here. Please let me know how it goes. I am happy for you.

# 5

I am glad to see you back. I was thinking about some things while you were gone. I wanted to share it with you.

## I think you are amazing.

We are in this together and I have a plan.

I was spending some time while you were away working on self care.

I used a new charcoal facial and looked through some new books that I had ordered. Just spending some time with my stuff. You know how that goes.

I have always loved books and there is a new style out that is mostly poetry. I am really enjoying them but feel like something is missing.

Maybe it is just me.

So where were we? Covering our bases

when it comes to self love, selfish people, relationships and dealing with who we are.

After all, we are here. It is an amazing

miracle.
Something happened in one split second and you were created.
How does that make you feel?
Do you feel worthy? You are.

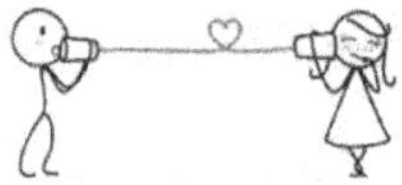

I wanted you to get that message.
Find your true self again. Right now.
It is going to take a lot of practice to really feel the miracle of who you are.
Things are getting ready to change for you.
All you need is to walk your path with pride and the feeling of love for all humans. Trust me it will work.

When you find that place inside of you that gets it, share this book with someone that may enjoy it. I am so glad that you are here and are taking the time now to care for yourself and fulfill your hopes and dreams.

Pay it forward

# 6

So let's take a break. All of this work trying to fix ourselves can be tiring. I have been putting in an extra effort to truly get it and put it all into play as quickly as possible.

What's your plan?

Will you work less and play more? Love more and love yourself even more?

## Please do.

You need to do this for yourself.

Your family or future family will understand.
They will see you glowing with love you give out and take in.
Can you feel it yet?

I can.

Ok. Break over.
That was nice.

So where were we? I wanted to tell you a story about how I got to be here.

Our story of how it all began is part of who we are.
I was born in Illinois.
I had wonderful grandparents and was always encouraged to make-believe different life scenarios. Which may have made me super creative.

You may hear me say some great things about myself and I hope that it does not make you think differently of me. We should love who we are. I want you to toot your own horn.
Everyday.

Let the world know how amazing you are.

They all need to know.
There is only one of you.
You are needed here and will always be
remembered for your talents.
Ahh, I see.
You may think that you do not have the
talents you desire.
Talents and goals are not in the stuff
category so this should be easy.
Try something. Anything.
What is it that interests you?
Write it down.
Fall in love with yourself.
You are pretty awesome.

There I go tooting your horn again. I hope you don't mind.
I just want you to be happy.

So just to back up a moment. I had lots of dreams when I was young.
Sometimes it was so bad that my teachers took notice. I had all of these ideas and inventions. I loved fairy tales.

Little did I know that ten years later nothing would change.
Twenty years later still nothing.
Thirty came and went.

Still trying.

Years and years went by. I could have been anything.
I did not know that.

Hey Universe! I got to be here!
I am sending out my wishes to you!
Please reply.

Nothing.

Where do all of those wishes go?

More Years go by and still the ideas keep piling up but none of them come to life. No big inventions or ideas made me famous.
I did not have a Cinderella Wedding.
I did not get a law degree or become a doctor.
My hair was too thin and straggly.
My glasses were too big.
My legs were too long.

None of the ideals I had about myself were true.

I could have had every single one of those things. My problem was that I did not know that I could. I did not know that if I stopped dreaming about it and believed in myself enough to take action that something

I felt strongly about could have come to life.

I had no idea.

I was here. I was enough. I gave up.

I didn't even know that I did it. I just always thought nothing ever worked right for me. Poor choices. The wrong jobs. The wrong relationships.
When my path was changing I did not see the signs and follow it.

I stayed on the wrong path trying to fix it. Trying to give something I did not have to stay normal. To stay the same.

I have no idea why I did that. I did not want to stay that way.

I had the dreams. And they floated away as quickly as I thought of another one. Like that would help.

The first dream was good but I let it go. I was not capable. I did not believe in myself. I did not realize that just by being here that anything was possible.

What is your dream? You have got to get that dream into play.
My first dream came true way too late in life.
It came true because someone told me I could do it.
It was that easy.

I was at work and I had an idea.
Someone looked at me and said do it!
I replied with a quick...what? Just do it?

Is it really that easy? Yes.

But maybe I was filled with doubt and

**A**s soon as someone gave me permission to live the dream and go after my idea.... I was crazy.

**I** spent day and night thinking about it. I told others. I wrote it all down.
Why didn't someone tell me this before?
All I needed was someone to say those few little words and my life changed.

**O**f course as your dreams start to come true you will grow.
You will change.

**Y**ou will love yourself even more.

**Y**ou will love the world and others just a little more everyday.

Life changes and piles favors on you that you could not imagine.

Permission granted!

Just do it.

What is your dream?

Today is the day. It is your day.
Do not give up.
Giving up is not an option.

You keep going until the dream is complete and then you start the next.
This is the only chance we get.
Well, unless you become a butterfly but I promised not to mention that again so I won't.

Be true to yourself. Take care of yourself.

BUILD your Dream and walk your path in life with every ounce of you there is.

You can do this!

# 7

Let's do something special. I am so happy that you are still here with me. We made it all of the way to Chapter Seven together and I am enjoying your company.

I had a very special day. I thought about you. I spent time filling up my heart with giving. It is important to keep yourself full of this. I know you must be tired from the rituals of day to day life but you can do this.

It will feel good. I helped someone today that was sleeping on a sidewalk. He was alone with his service dog. People stopped and looked at me sitting there with the man. How rude of me to acknowledge him. I accepted him for who he was. We talked and played with his dog. I gave him things from my car.

Acceptance in life is important. Accepting our idea of flaws in others who are perfect in their own truth. Get it? These flaws only exist in us. When you let that go you can see their perfection.

I really feel the importance of changing something in this world everyday. There has got to be something we can do.

I have spent time scooping up worms off of hot sidewalks by getting them to the grass safely. I have jumped over the ant hill.

The little things in life are the amazing things. Walk your path proudly as a kind human and do it regardless of what others think.

I hope this all helps. I hope you are feeling the love of this little book and that you're glowing with self love and the love for others. I have not found any reason to not be this way.

So while traveling your path think of this. A wise man once said, “How are you living?” Think about that for a moment. Go all of the way back if you need to. How are you living? Say it again. Sometimes I forget. When I really start to think about my life over and over again I remind myself that I am living my life. I got to be here. Here we are. That does not seem like a big deal but it is. There are so many people that have not had the chance to be here.

Right now there are others fighting for their lives. Some have just lost theirs. Some would give anything to get one more day to see a smile or give one. Are you that person?

An important part of seeing the big picture is asking yourself each day the question. How are you living? Do you wake up each day thankful? Do you find something good to be thankful for?

It is hard to keep focus. It is hard to see the end result of our good work. I know that it will be ok. But why does it have to be so hard? If I go back to the original train of thought it would be a never ending circle. I want stuff. I want to be happy. I want to make others happy. I feel sad that nothing goes my way. I feel lonely. I wish I was someone else.

We are dancing in the circle again. I am no professional. Just a girl. I am just me. Someone that always wanted to live big dreams and then feel bad when they never came to life.

If only someone would have told me that I could do it. I needed permission to live a life that was not mine. Because in all reality right now we are living our life. This very moment we are here.

Take a moment. Here it is. The day has come. We are here to live this day. Yes it is important to plan sometimes for years to come. But spending all of your time planning is not really living. Live today. Right now. Do every single thing that you sit there and dream of.

Try to find some perspective on this though.

Dive into life.

Love freely.

Give yourself your best.

How are you living? After all

... you got to be here!

I hope that you are ok. I hope that you can listen to your inner voice that is telling you to be happy. Not that you are not already happy but can you really be too happy? Constant happiness is great and it can be annoying to others around us sometimes.

You may hear, "Why the heck is she so happy all of the time?" or "How can he be so happy with his job?" There will always be someone that will steal your joy. The word joy is right there with happy. Those two words will get you through the most trying times. They will also lead you down the path of a complete life that you never miss a moment of.

# HAPPY

The word that can fix it all. Here we are.

We are planning on great happiness.

The happy feeling is here.
No one is taking it away.
Happiness becomes greater.

Still guarding it.
It is growing into even more
happiness.

I think we may be onto something
here.
I am really happy to meet you.
I am happy to be here with you.
How are you feeling right now?

I know it has been hard. It is a
tough world out there.
But we are all in this together.

# 8

I see it. The look on your face. You are making a crooked lip at me or raising your eyebrow. How will this ever work? Is it really that simple?

The way that I see it yes. Yes it will work. I think there are so many of us that want to make a difference and beat the odds of having a sad and lonely life. We want to change the world. We want to be thankful we are here. We want stuff. Lol. Yup. I had to go there.

I am not sure where this will all lead right away but let's do something great together. Let's get online and be a group of new happy and encouraging friends.

The info will be on the last page. I hope to see you there after we are done here. Maybe if there are enough of us we can go to the beach. Or rent a cruise ship. Let's do something fun. At the same time we will build up each other's dreams and enjoy this moment we have.

I love this moment. It is actually one of my favorites. I did what they said could not be done. I wrote about my life and yours too. I wanted to tell you that I am happy you got to be here.

Why the long face?

Has it been hard?

My husband left me. My kids left home. I lost my job. I never surfed. I lost my best friend. I have been sick. I feel lonely. I am sad. My stove broke. My car is old.

I need a new couch. My dog ran away. My cat is old. I am old. I want to be young again. I am too thin. I am too big. I am too tall. I am too short. My teeth hurt. My glasses are broken. No one loves me.

## Write your own here:

---

Well you may feel right about some of those things. But you are wrong about one.

Someone does love you. It is yourself and well maybe I do too.

I have a lot of love to give. I am sure that you do too.

Let's find a way to share it all and be happy again.

I know we can.

But first in order to do that we have to

eliminate the crap. You know that toxic sludge that is keeping us down.

From this day forward I will walk away from the bull.

Being around people that bring you down

instead of building you up is a waste of time.
Remember, the path is short.

There will always be humans that have

only one purpose in life and that is to hurt others and strip them of their dreams.

Do you feel bare?

Standing there like that will only catch you a cold.

**Be fearless in the pursuit of what sets your soul on fire!**

Now you are getting it!
It is all about you!

# 9

We are getting closer. I feel it. It is almost time for this little book to end.

I hope it helped. I hope that it made a difference for you.

I know that you are wonderful and amazing and awesome.

I am sure we can get through this together

and enjoy every moment of this life that we have. After all, we are pretty lucky to be here.
It is actually a miracle.

Because we are perfect and going to be ok.

I am sure of it.

I hope you noticed. I skipped a page.

I didn't do it for myself, I did it for you.
Do you love it?

It is a special page.
Just like you.

Maybe you want to write something there.
Or maybe you don't.

Is there something troubling you?
I know that sometimes there are not enough words to tell someone that it will be ok. Sometimes there is no hope.

Where can you get it? Not online or at the store that is for sure.
But you can get it. It is inside of you and if I have read the directions correctly, this hope is easy to whip up.

People will say you can actually just sit there and make some hope. It could magically appear right inside of you. I see that the directions also say that to avoid a chance of losing hope, you should surround yourself with other humans that really want you to have the hope. They can help you make more.

If you run out of ingredients do not give up.
The recipe itself is simple to find.

I promise it is better than any recipe you have ever seen.

Let's do it together.
You know. Rise up and be strong.
Find our happiness and joy.
Be ourselves and be loved for it.
After all, you are perfect.
You know that.
And I love you.

I feel like I might start missing you

right now.
A few years ago I had said to myself that you could not miss someone that you did not know.
I think I was incorrect.

There is a feeling there.
A feeling that we are all connected and this connection is going to bring us all together to a place filled with love and friendship.

How do I know this?

Because I have been waiting for you all of my years.
I was lonely too.
Sometimes I felt like nobody would ever love me.
Not like the way I see real love happen.

But wait! It's all about you!

# It's all about me!

If you want to get the recipe.
If you want to find yourself.
If you want to be yourself!
Come on over!
Let's meet.
I will be waiting on my facebook page.
It is the only place I know to go
where you can find me.
We can focus on the good things in
life.
Talk about our dreams.
Talk about how we lucked out and got
to be here.
Because we did.
I did and I love this day.
This is the day.
Our day.

## I got to be here.

Here we are at the end.
Every SINGLE DAY I am grateful to be here.

Wake up each day and sincerely appreciate the miracle behind the moment.

I am here. I got to be here. My heart is filled with gratitude for every moment that I get to enjoy on this planet.

# The End

But not really. It is just the
beginning.
You got this

You're perfectly designed

You're enough

And YOU GOT TO BE HERE

I know we can find each other again
by using some simple ways.
I want to know you.
I want others to know you!
If you are online

Use

A hashtag. It is a little # symbol
before a word.
#IGottoBeHere
Keep the words together.
Use it online.
Use it on Facebook, Twitter and
Instagram
I will be there.
So will others just like us that want
to be happy again.
Nice humans.

I got to

be Here

Other books by Deb Stratton
Then I was gone
ALIEN ZOO

Urban Bigfoot
Urban Bigfoot 2
Urban Bigfoot Em's Journal

The Bigfoot Farm  A childrens Book

Witches Night Out Spell Book
SANDY
I got to Be here

The Honey Cabin

URBAN BIGFOOT SERIES
BOOKS 1-6

A few more I will tell you about later :)

Where can you find them?
On Amazon
Search up Deb Stratton or Debbie
Barnes & Noble
Books a Million
Jet.com Walmart.com

They are all in more than twenty languages so pick one :)

And thank you for being here.

Love,

Deb

Follow me on Facebook
@DebStratton Author
@Igottobehere

# Love,
# Deb

www.ingramcontent.com/pod-product-compliance
Lightning Source LLC
Chambersburg PA
CBHW052119150726
48002CB00006B/2412
* 9 7 9 8 6 8 0 6 6 6 1 1 1 *